THE CAT'S STORY

A PET'S RECORD BOOK

I have studied many philosophers and many cats. The wisdom of
cats is infinitely superior.

Hippolyte Taine (1828–93)

For I am possessed of a cat, surpassing in beauty,
from whom I take occasion to bless Almighty God.

Christopher Smart (1722–71)

THE CAT'S STORY

A PET'S RECORD BOOK

COMPILED BY CELIA HADDON

PAVILION
PRODUCTIONS

THIS BOOK BELONGS TO

Your cat is loved and wanted. Please remember unwanted, lost and abused cats and kittens by supporting animal rescue charities and the Cats Protection League.

First published in 1991 by Pavilion Productions Ltd
A division of Pavilion Books Ltd
196 Shaftesbury Avenue, London WC2H 8JL
Copyright © Text and selection of illustrations Celia Haddon 1991
Copyright © Design and concept Pavilion Productions Ltd 1991
Designed by Ron Pickless
Typeset by P&M Typesetting
Printed and bound in Italy by New Interlitho

ISBN 1 85145 601 5

A CELEBRATION

Cats bring joy and beauty and love into our lives. With graceful steps they cross the gulf that divides animals from humans, to become part of our family. Yet in doing so they lose nothing of their own mysterious individuality.

This book provides a record of a special friendship – a loving bond between you and your cat. In these pages you can trace the growth of your relationship and write a life story of your cat. A cat is never really owned, but if we are a friend to a cat, it will be a friend to us. And this special friendship is not to be undertaken lightly. When we buy a new pedigree kitten, give a home to an unwanted little waif from the cat's home or rescue a forsaken stray cat off the street, we are taking on the responsibility for another being's happiness.

To care for a cat is a privilege. Cats do not bestow their trust easily. Their love and faith go only to human beings who are worthy of them. Their friendship has to be deserved.

And each relationship is different. There are outgoing cats who fling themselves fearlessly into the human family, happy to be a careless playfellow of all its members. There are shy cats who will retreat from affection offered too clumsily. There are cats with a mysterious charm and cats with the cunning vitality of the streets.

This book celebrates your own cat's life and special character.

How to Use This Book

This book is first of all a keepsake of your cat. But it will also be of practical use to cat lovers. With its entries for vet's address and a next-of-kin telephone number, it can accompany your cat to boarding catteries. The detailed breakdown of your cat's diet and food preferences will help them give proper care. Or it can be handed to a cat sitter, who needs to know the details of your cat's daily routine and grooming.

It will also act as a reminder about health care. The written record of your cat's health, its vaccinations, and any illnesses can prompt your memory when visiting the vet.

But it is much more than that. This book will allow you to preserve the loving moments of a friendship. When your cat is a grave and stately feline, you will be able to recall the playful pranks of its kittenhood with the help of these pages. There are two pages for photographs to recall your cat's changing appearance.

There is room for you to write down the special moments that would otherwise be forgotten. There is space to record your feelings about your feline friend and a page for your cat to contribute its pawmark, if it should choose to do so.

And this keepsake has another use. The heartbreak of loving a cat is that it lives such a shorter time than we do. Memories often fade with the years. This album will help you keep fresh the memory of a very special friend.

He is in youth swift, pliant and merry, and leapeth and rusheth on
all thing that is before him; and is lead by a straw and playeth
therewith.

Bartholomaeus Anglicus *De Proprietatibus Rerum* (1398)

Names

My cat's name

Why I chose this name

Nicknames, loving names and kitten names

Can he name a kitten? By this test I am condemned, for I cannot.

Samuel Butler (1835–1902)

PEDIGREE NAME OR ORIGINAL NAME

The cat is truly an aristocrat in type and origin.

Alexandre Dumas (1802–70)

How I found my cat

Why I chose my cat

The first time I saw my new cat

I love little pussy,
Her coat is so warm,
And if I don't hurt her,
She'll do me no harm.

Nursery rhyme

MY CAT'S LIFE BEFORE WE MET

The playful kitten with its pretty little tigerish gambol is infinitely more amusing than half the people one is obliged to live with in the world.

Lady Sydney Morgan (1783–1859)

A Portrait of My Cat

BREED OR TYPE

COLOURING

SPECIAL MARKS

COLOUR OF EYES

TYPE OF FUR

Nothing is more playful than a young cat,
nor more grave than an old one.

Thomas Fuller (1608–61)

O lovely Pussy, O Pussy, my love,
What a beautiful pussy you are,
You are,
You are!
What a beautiful pussy you are.

Edward Lear (1812–88)

First Days

The date and time my cat arrived

The first days of settling in

I have a kitten, the drollest of creatures that ever wore a cat's skin. She is dressed in a tortoiseshell suit and I know that you will delight in her.

William Cowper (1731–1800)

I'll not pull her tail,
Nor drive her away,
But pussy and I
Very gently will play.

Nursery rhyme

MY NEW CAT'S PHOTOGRAPH

Such a light of gladness breaks,
Pretty kitten! from thy freaks.

William Wordsworth (1770–1850)

MORE ABOUT MY NEW CAT

A PAWPRINT

A LOCK OF HAIR

PET REGISTRY DETAILS

If I lost my little cat, I should be sad without it.
I should ask St Jerome what to do about it.
I should ask St Jerome, just because of that
He's the only saint I know that kept a pussy cat.

Children's rhyme

My Cat and I

The humans in our family

The animals in our family

Family members who come to stay

If man could be crossed with a cat, it would improve man
but deteriorate the cat.

Mark Twain (1835–1910)

I like cats and dogs very much indeed. They are much superior to
human beings as companions. They never say unkind things.

Jerome K. Jerome (1859–1927)

Early Days

A day in the life of my cat – from breakfast to night time

See the kitten on the wall,
Sporting with the leaves that fall…
But the kitten how she starts,
Crouches, stretches, paws and darts.

William Wordsworth (1770–1850)

God has blessed him in the variety of his movements.

Christopher Smart (1722–71)

Early Ways

Favourite games

Favourite toys

Favourite hiding places

Favourite sleeping places

This beast is wonderful nimble, setting upon her prey like a lion, by leaping.

Edward Topsell (1572–1625)

How she beggeth, playeth, leapeth, looketh, catcheth, tosseth
with her foot, riseth up to strings held over her head, sometimes
creeping, sometimes lying on the back, playing with one foot...

Edward Topsell (1572–1625)

Health

My cat's first visit to the vet

Name and address of vet

Insurance details

Details of operation

Cats, by means of their whiskers, seem to possess something like
an additional sense: these have perhaps, some analogy to
the antennae of moths and butterflies.

Rev. W. Bingley *Animal Biography* (1829)

Vaccination Dates and Details

Doubtless cats talk and reason with one another.

Izaak Walton (1593–1683)

Illnesses
Date and Details

Strength must be maintained from the very commencement
by frequent small doses of strong beef tea.

Harrison Weir *Our Cats* (1889)

A cat is much delighted to play with her image in a glass, and if at
any time she behold it in water, presently she leapeth down into
the water which naturally she doth abhor. Nothing is more
contrary to the nature of a cat than is wet and water and for this
cause came the proverb that they love not to wet their feet.

Edward Topsell (1572–1625)

Beauty Care

Brushing

Fleas and other creepies

Nail manicure and teeth care

It is a neat and cleanly creature, often licking itself to keep it
fair and clean, and washing its face with its fore feet.

William Salmon (1644–1713)

WEIGHTS AND DATES

She useth therefore to wash her face with her feet, which she
licketh and moisteneth with her tongue; and it is observed by some
that if she put her feet beyond the crown of her head in this
kind of washing, it is a sign of rain.

John Swan *Speculum Mundi* (1643)

My Cat's Hobbies

Games with humans

Hunting or chasing games

Other hobbies

When I am playing with my cat, who knows whether she have more
sport in dallying with me than I have in gaming with her? We
entertain one another with mutual apish tricks.

Michel Montaigne (1533–92)

The cat is domestic only as far as it suits its own ends.

Hector Munro, 'Saki' (1870–1916)

My Cat's Menu

DAILY FOOD

MEAL TIMES

FAVOURITE FOOD

WHERE MY CAT EATS

When the tea is brought in at five o'clock,
And all the neat curtains are drawn with care,
The little black cat with bright green eyes
Is suddenly purring there

Harold Monro (1879–1932)

Treats

Favourite treats

Let take a cat and foster him well with milk
And tender flesh and make his couch of silk,
And let him see a mouse go by the wall,
Anon he waveth milk and flesh and all,
And every dainty that is in that house,
Such appetite he hath to eat a mouse.

Geoffrey Chaucer (1345–1400)

My Cat's Holiday

CATTERIES

WHAT TO PACK

CAT SITTERS

NEXT OF KIN ADDRESSES FOR EMERGENCIES

Ah! Cats are a mysterious kind of folk. There is more passing
in their minds than we are aware of.

Sir Walter Scott (1771–1832)

Pussy cat, pussy cat, where have you been?
I've been up to London to visit the Queen.

Nursery rhyme

My Cat's Likes and Dislikes

Favourite caresses

Clever tricks

Words my cat understands

Naughty behaviour

Hates and fears

For he purrs in thankfulness, when God tells him he's a good cat.

Christopher Smart (1722–71)

Cats consider theft a game,
And, howsoever you may blame,
Refuse the slightest sign of shame.

Anonymous

FRIENDS AND FOES

HUMAN FRIENDS

HUMAN FOES

ANIMAL FRIENDS

ANIMAL FOES

What cat was ever awkward or clumsy? Whether in play or in
earnest, cats are the very embodiment of elegance.

Charles H. Ross *The Book of Cats* (1868)

D is for Dog, steadfast, honest and true;
I hope he gets married to Pussy, don't you?

Victorian alphabet book

My Cat at Home

Look-out places

Places to nap

Hiding places

I have (and long shall have) a white, great, nimble cat.
A king upon a mouse, a strong foe to the rat.

Sir Philip Sidney (1554–86)

SCRATCHING PLACES

PLACES TO EXPLORE

A house without a cat, and a well-fed, well-petted, and properly
revered cat, may be a perfect house perhaps, but how
can it prove its title?

Mark Twain (1835–1910)

IMPORTANT MOMENTS IN MY CAT'S LIFE

Few animals exhibit more maternal tenderness, or show a greater
love for their offspring, than the cat.

Rev. W. Bingley *Animal Biography* (1829)

The Egyptians have observed in the eyes of a cat,
the increase of the moonlight.

Edward Topsell (1572–1625)

Anniversaries and Special Dates

There is nothing sweeter than his peace when at rest.
For there is nothing brisker than his life when in motion.

Christopher Smart (1722–71)

Stately, kindly, lordly friend,
Condescend
Here to sit by me, and turn
Glorious eyes that smile and burn,
Golden eyes, love's lustrous meed,
On the golden page I read.

Algernon Charles Swinburne (1837–1909)

MY FAVOURITE PHOTOGRAPH

When the moon gets up and night comes, he is the cat that walks by
himself, and all places are alike to him.

Rudyard Kipling (1865–1936)

FAVOURITE MEMORIES

His purr, when he purred for sheer happiness of life, was as the purr of many kettles.

Oswald Barron (1836–1939)

Pet was never mourned as you,
Purrer of the spotless hue,
Plumy tail and wistful gaze,
While you humoured our queer ways.

Thomas Hardy (1840–1928)